Step-by-Step
Relief
Carving

by David Bennett and Roger Schroeder

Fox
Chapel Publishing Co. Inc.

1970 Broad Street • East Petersburg, PA 17520 • www.foxchapelpublishing.com

Dedication

To my parents, Denny and Betty, for without their support and encouragement this book could not be possible, from David

To Sheila, whose eyes for details are surpassed by none, from Roger

Publisher	Alan Giagnocavo
Project Editor	Ayleen Stellhorn
Desktop Specialist	Linda Eberly, Eberly Designs Inc.
Cover Design	Keren Holl

ISBN #1–56523–101–5
Library of Congress Preassigned Card Number: 2002102661

To order your copy of this book,
please send check or money order
for the cover price plus $3.00 shipping to:
Fox Books
1970 Broad Street
East Petersburg, PA 17520

Or visit us on the web at
www.foxchapelpublishing.com

Manufactured in Korea
10 9 8 7 6 5 4 3 2 1

Table of Contents

About the Authors

David Bennett

David Bennett began his career in woodcarving while studying for his bachelor of fine arts degree at Edinboro University of Pennsylvania in 1976. While developing his art, he became interested in boatbuilding, sailmaking and ship carving. Eventually he combined his formal education in sculpture with nine years of practical experience as a boatbuilder and sailmaker.

David's unique style of woodcarving combines the theory of a painter and the tools of a sculptor to create an art form that goes beyond traditional low relief. Treating the carving as if it were a monochromatic painting, he uses wood and light to create the values and contrast needed to condense the third dimension of his sculptures.

In 1986, he started Falls Run Woodcarving, primarily as a custom carving shop and woodcarving school. David and a former student, Rich Reimers, began to develop a new type of flexible carving tool Rich had been making in his basement. The unconventional design allowed the tool to be multi-functional, and a carver was able to reach into recessed areas without having to change tools. Students began using the tools almost exclusively. In 1991, production began under the trademark Flexcut™ carving tools and is now sold internationally under David's direction of the Flexcut Tool Co. Inc. in Erie, Pennsylvania.

Roger Schroeder

Roger Schroeder's success as a writer began when he gave up trying to write the great American novel. Instead, he turned to writing about his hobby: woodworking. While sharpening his writing skills and photography, he expanded his interests and went on to author 16 books and hundreds of magazine articles. Ranging in scope from woodcarving to housebuilding, the books include *How to Carve Wildfowl, Carving Signs, Making Toys,* Timber Frame Construction, and *Scrimshaw.* He is also founding and managing editor of *Wood Carving Illustrated* magazine.

Roger lectures on a variety of wood-related topics: furniture, houses, and wood sculpture. In the remaining time he is an amateur cabinetmaker—specializing in Victorian reproductions—and a bird carver who has received a number of blue ribbons for his natural wood sculptures.

Roger lives with his wife Sheila in Amityville, New York.

Introduction

by David Bennett

Throughout the years that I have been practicing art, I have become most familiar with relief sculpture. Even though it has been around since 10,000 B.C., it is a relatively unexplored art form today. Over the centuries, most artists have used it to embellish functional objects such as doors and vessels. Relief is the combination of two disciplines of art: painting as a two-dimensional discipline and sculpture as a three-dimensional discipline. A combination of the two is not always very logical and can prove to be quite a challenge.

My interest in art began not with relief work but with drawing. When I was five years old I stumbled onto a way of "seeing" that allowed me to draw fairly well for a child. At that time I won an art contest on a television show that is now known as "Mr. Roger's Neighborhood." It was not what I would call a major coupe in the art world, but it did two very important things for me. First, it gave me the incentive to continue with my interest in art. Second, it persuaded my parents to encourage me.

After graduating from art school in 1976, I had a wide range of occupations, many of which did not involve what most people would call art. In 1985, I read *Drawing on the Right Side of the Brain* by Betty Edwards. It explained in scientific terms a way of seeing that allows you to draw well; and it demonstrated the process with accompanying pencil exercises so that you can prove it to yourself. In 1994, I took a class from her in New York. Although I could draw with reasonable assurance, the majority of the 60 other student were novices at best. In a period of five days I watched in amazement as these students became skilled enough at

drawing for each to complete, in a matter of hours, a self-portrait most anyone would be envious of.

Drawing is a skill to be learned and practiced just as you would learn to read and write. The harder you work, the more talented you become at the skill. My skills as a woodcarver increased proportionately with my skills in drawing. As a result, I achieved greater control over my powers of observation instead of greater control over my carving tools. Hopefully, some of my observations about how relief carving works will aid you in your own creations. Although wood is used as the medium, the principles work for other materials. The real challenge is mixing an equal amount of desire and time to practice.

Art helps us to exercise our creative ability in all endeavors. Without being able to use information creatively, whether in math, science or some other pursuit, we are consigned to the status quo.

T.A. Ivy, 31 in. by 22 in. by 2 in., cherry, 1985
The undercutting of the boom and seagull allows light to flow behind them. The rigging is added. Since the rigging is attached going across the grain and glued at both ends, it has the problem of breaking loose as the summer humidity expands the wood. Notice how the grain of the wood in the sky moves into the sail of the boat, giving it a transparent effect. The style of boat pictured is the Cape Cod catboat. The rigging's shape and style comprise truly American designs.

Coastwise Fishing, 46 in. by 31 in. by 2 in., Honduras mahogany, 1984
The composition was my first serious attempt at relief carving after experimenting with it in college. After spending many hours drawing the image directly on the wood, I soon learned that it took only a few moments to remove it with a gouge. The lesson I learned was the importance of having an original paper copy as a reference.

Step-by-Step Relief Carving

Gallery

This gallery section is included to show the chronological development of my work. Carving each piece was a learning experience necessary for carving the next one. As you will notice, I have an interest in maritime themes. Most of the subjects include a historical study of a particular boat or ship and how it was used. The wine-glass shapes framing many of the images are reproductions of the boats' transoms that are in the compositions. The frames are intended to endow a crystal-ball effect. However, instead of looking into the future, they help us look into our maritime heritage.

— David Bennett

The Wherry, 23 in. by 18 in. by 2 in. Honduras mahogany, cedar and oak, 1986
The extreme foreshortening of the boat contributes to the visual sense of depth even though it is only 2 in. thick. However, the clouds are carved without perspective and tend to flatten the look of the sky. There is an absence of clouds in later pieces because of this effect. Only as I became familiar with drawing clouds do they appear in more recent compositions.

▲ *The Flying Set*, 33 in. by 25 in. by 2 in., Honduras mahogany, 1986
The image illustrates that dories were launched from the deck of fishing schooners while underway. It uses extreme foreshortening to achieve visual depth. The rigging has been added, running parallel to the grain. This technique allowed it to remain completely intact as the wood expands and contracts with the seasons.

▼

▲ *Chesapeake Bay Log Canoes*, 37 in. by 19 in. by 2 in.,
Honduras mahogany, 1987
A racing canoe was kept from capsizing by positioning its
crew on long planks that were extended over the rail, thus
acting as a counterbalance to the force of the wind. The
typical hull was constructed from a series of logs that were
doweled together side by side. The outside shape, as well
as the hollow inside, was carved with axes and adzes.
Final smoothing was completed with a wood plane to
"fair" the hull.

Sandbagger Shuffle, 46 in. by 18 in. by 2 in., Honduras
mahogany, 1987
The Sandbagger is tilted in the composition as it was often
observed on the water. The over-canvassed racer used up
to two tons of sandbags stacked on the windward side of
the boat to keep it upright. In order to successfully tack or
change direction, the sandbags needed to be shifted from
one side of the boat to the other before the turn was completed to reduce the risk of capsizing. Teamwork and speed
were vital, and the shuffle became organized chaos. ▼

Stalwarts, 26 in. by 24 in. by 2 in., Honduras mahogany, 1988
The challenge of this carving was to see if a ship as complex as a square-rigged barque could be completed with the techniques I had developed to date. The scene takes place in Gloucester, Massachusetts, circa 1880. It was a period when sail, steam and oar were all commercially viable forms of water propulsion.

Sportin' the Rod, 25 in. by 19 in. by 2 in., Honduras mahogany, 1988
Contrast plays an important role in depth perception. Notice how each consecutive layer of the landscape has a different amount of contrast, decreasing toward the background. The foreground has deep black and white highlights. The mountains in the extreme background exhibit much less range between black and white. High-gloss varnish was applied on the water portions of the image to create glare and in turn increase the highlighting.

▲ *Erie Public Dock* Circa 1888, 48 in. by 32 in. by 2 in., Honduras mahogany, 1989
Primarily a historical study of my hometown's waterfront, it is the largest relief carving I've done to date. The Erie boat shown in the foreground was indigenous to Lake Erie and first used as a tender for a fixed fish trap called a pound net.

The Bailer, 33 in. by 26 in. by 2 in., Honduras mahogany, 1989
Sailing small craft single-handedly can be somewhat arduous, especially in a rising breeze. As the waves begin to splash over the side and the boat up fills with more and more water, bailing becomes more important than steering. Sometimes the nearest beach is the best place to handle the problem. I attempted to capture the sense of wind and wave, using the flogging sail and a changing wave structure. ▼

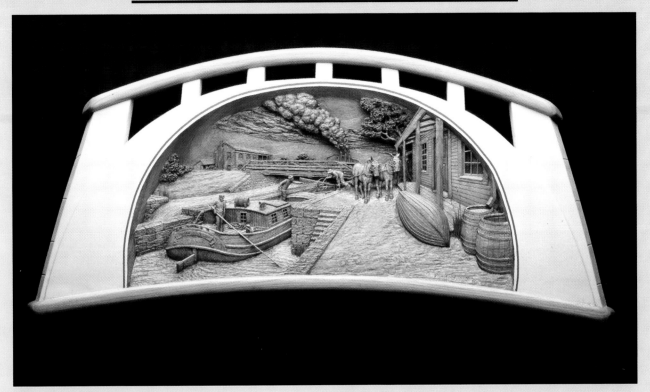

▲ **The Hoggee's Tow**, 37 in. by 20 in. by 2 in., Honduras mahogany, 1990

The canal period in our history is often overlooked because much of the evidence of its existence—the canals—has been filled in. Canals once stretched deep into our heartland and acted as the first real transportation network. The term "hoggee" is an old Scottish word for laborer. It became a generic term for the person driving the mules that pulled the canal boat along its journey. The "tow" is the rope that connected the two. Hoggees were often runaway or delinquent children who slept along with the mules. James Garfield, our 20th president, was once a hoggee on a canal.

Silent Virtue, 23 in. by 16 in. by 2 in., Honduras mahogany, 1990

Scow schooners once delivered everything from hay to lumber. When the wind died, the only resource for propulsion was the yawl boat carried on the stern. It was a daunting task to tow 60 tons of schooner through the water with a pair of oars, but with the determination of an ant, the scow began to move slowly on until the breeze came up again. Carving the piece was an exercise in contrast and atmosphere. The yawl boat in the foreground is carved deeply and the scow schooner is carved very shallow to make it less visible, thus creating a sense of fog.

The Iron Steamer, 28 in. by 19 in. by 2 in., Honduras mahogany, 1991

The U.S.S. Michigan was the first iron battleship built for the United States Navy and was constructed in Erie, Pennsylvania in 1843. It cruised The Great Lakes to keep amity between the United States and Canada after the War of 1812. It never once fired a shot in battle from its only cannon in its more than 80 years in commission. It is shown here leaving Presque Isle Bay around 1876 under its auxiliary power of steam and sidewheel as the sails are being unfurled for open water. Smoke from the coal-fired boiler would flow from its stack and eventually cover the white canvas sails with black soot.

CHAPTER ONE

Light and the Illusion of Relief

One of the most common problems novice relief carvers have in creating a complex composition is running out of wood as they dig deeper and deeper, trying to achieve the desired effect of visual depth. Often this results from trying to carve objects in the composition almost entirely in the round.

To prevent this kind of frustration, it is important to first understand how our brain uses light to perceive objects as three-dimensional. This understanding will show you how to use the visual illusion of depth.

There are two terms which need to be defined in order to grasp this idea. One is the color value of an object. *Value* is the property of a color by which it is distinguished as light or dark, ie: dark red or light red. The other is *contrast* and is defined by how varied the range of values are in a composition. For example, the sight of a polar bear in a snowstorm will have little contrast while a flashlight seen in a dark night will have a lot. Our brain associates objects that have a wider range of values with being more three-dimensional.

To better illustrate this, look at the eggs in Figure 1:1. One is a real egg and the other is a white egg-shaped piece of paper. Which one has a wider range of values? Which one appears more three-dimensional?

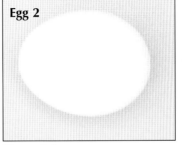

Figure 1:2

Keeping this in mind, you can use the direction of the light source to control how dimensional the real egg appears. Egg 1 is illuminated with a light source coming from the side to yield greater contrast and dimension. In Figure 1:2, Egg 2 is the same object illuminated from directly in front. Notice that the shadows are washed away and the egg appears flatter than the prior situation.

Now that you have seen how lighting an object from the side enhances shadows to create a sense of depth, take a look at how adding highlights and removing shadows trick the eye further.

Fooling the Eye

Figure 1:3 shows a carved duck. Notice the way the light interacts with it. Shadows are cast on and under the body. There are also places where the light flows behind it and shadows are non-existent. All of these

Figure 1:1

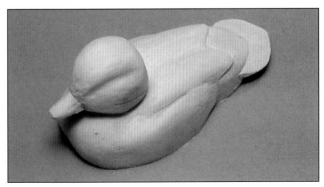

Figure 1:3

qualities work together to convince your brain that it is a picture of an in-the-round sculpture.

Figure 1:4 shows two ducks. One is the three-dimensional sculpture, the other is the same duck cut in half along its length and attached to a background. Notice the shadows under the bill and tail feathers of the half duck in comparison to the other. These different shadows allow you to tell them apart.

In Figure 1:5 the half duck is pulled away from its background and light is allowed to flow behind it. The appearance of the two is now very similar. However, even though they resemble each other, their thicknesses can still be recognized by the shadow projected under their bodies. The full carving has a larger shadow that reveals its thickness in relation to its thinner counterpart.

In Figure 1:6 the carving on the left is only ½ in. thick and is carved to mimic the shadows on the half duck that is 2 in. thick. They appear to be almost identical in appearance. Both are pulled away from the background to allow light to flow behind them, creating an in-the-round effect. The same situation is created as seen with Figure 1:5; their thicknesses can only be recognized by the shadows under their bodies, with the thinner bird having a narrower shadow.

Figure 1:7 shows what happens if the shadows under the ducks are eliminated when all three carvings are put on a shelf. The result is an illusion that all three are the same thickness. It is not until the ducks are viewed from the top (Figure 1:8) that you can tell which duck is full-bodied, which is half-round, and which is relief. Unfortunately, relief only produces a visually correct image when viewed from the front.

The Step-by-Step project in this book may look like high relief, done in very thick wood, but it is not. Backcutting or partially removing wood from behind elements of the design allows light to flow behind roof lines, boats and trees, just as it did with the duck example. Unnatural shadows are eliminated. This is only one component that aids in the illusion of high relief in material that is less than two inches thick.

To create effective relief carvings, you must combine the three-dimensional effect of light and shadow with the two-dimensional illusion of perspective drawing. Owing to this combination, relief carving is often referred to as a two-and-a-half-dimensional art form. How to bring this combination to the discipline of carving is the subject of the next chapter.

Figure 1:4

Figure 1:5

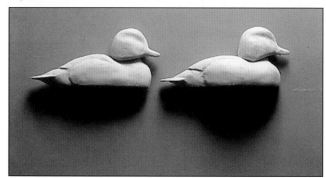

Figure 1:6

Figure 1:7

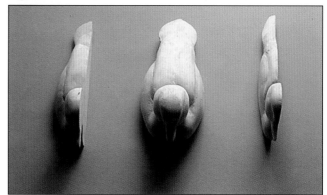

Figure 1:8

Step-by-Step Relief Carving

CHAPTER TWO

Combining Perspective with Light

Perspective is the technique that illustrates three-dimensional objects on a two-dimensional surface. You probably remember being introduced to perspective with a drawing of railroad tracks or telephone poles converging to a vanishing point on the horizon. The illusion of distance is quite effective. It is this illusion, when combined with carving techniques, that results in the kind of relief project offered in this book.

To begin to understand the concepts of perspective and light, look at the figures to the left. There are three versions of a drawn square or cube. The first square (Figure 2:1) is flat and has no visual dimension. The second (Figure 2:2) is a cube drawn in perspective, and it does have the illusion of depth, but light is not a factor. The lines only define where each of the surfaces starts and ends.

Figure 2:1

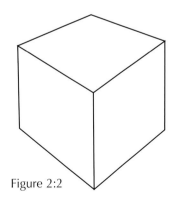

Figure 2:2

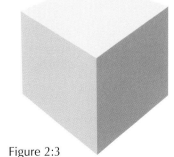

Figure 2:3

The third cube (Figure 2:3) is drawn with values. The property of a color by which it is distinguished as light or dark is a value. Think of the distinction, for example, between light red and dark red. This third cube is the most dimensional because a light source is introduced. Note that the lines are eliminated and that each surface is defined with a fill of various grays.

It will help your understanding of three dimensions to realize that lines do not exist in nature. They are merely mathematical concepts. If you look at different objects around your room, you will not see lines drawn on them defining their surfaces; instead, you see only colors and values of colors. To accomplish this in wood, you are going to use a variety of carving tools and a real light source instead of the side of a pencil to shade in a synthetic light source.

In Figure 2:4, a wooden cube is cut out to match the outline of the perspective drawing. Internal lines are drawn to define each surface. Just as the cube drawn with values (Figure 2:3) looks more dimensional, so too

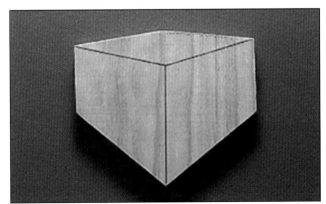

Figure 2:4

Step-by-Step Relief Carving

is the wooden cube. By carving wood away, the angle at which the light strikes each surface is manipulated. The lines act only as guides to show where to change the angles (Figure 2:5). Notice that the drawn lines are eliminated just as they are in the value drawing of the cube.

When viewing the cube from the side (Figure 2:6), you can see that the top of the cube is slanted back so that it reflects more light, giving it a "whiter" value. The sides of the cube are slanted down to the background, away from the light to give them a darker value. Having the source of light above and off to the sides allows for the three different values that are necessary to visualize the three sides. If the light source were directly in front of the cube, the contrast between the three sides as well as the perception of depth would be diminished.

It will be helpful to think of the carving as a monochromatic or "one color" painting in which white or black is added to that color to mix the different values needed to create the image. The one color designated for your carving is the color of the wood to which black or white is added. When white is needed, the surface is tilted toward the light. When black is needed, it is tilted away from the light.

Another important concept to note when viewing the cube from the side is the "tilting effect." Even though the sides are tilted to the background, the frontal appearance of the cube is not affected. From the front, the sides still have the illusion of being plum and vertical.

The effect of tilting serves two purposes in relief carving. For one, it eliminates the shadow under the cube that would otherwise expose the thickness of the wood, thus reducing the effect of perspective. Remember how eliminating this same type of shadow worked with the duck in the previous chapter (Figure 1:7). Also, if this shadow is not eliminated, the cube appears to float in the air. If an object were actually floating in the air, a shadow is cast on whatever it is floating above. Many beginning relief carvers forget this fact and will carve an object that is magically levitating above the ground. It may be a nice trick, but visually it is incorrect.

The second, and probably more important role the tilting effect serves is that it conserves the thickness of

the wood needed to create an entire composition where there are objects placed in front and behind each other. An image placed visually behind the cube by the use of perspective doesn't necessarily need to be physically carved at a deeper level.

The technique can also be applied to multiple images. Figure 2:7 shows a cube visually placed behind another using the same horizon line of the perspective drawing. Notice that there is no shadow cast on the top

Figure 2:5

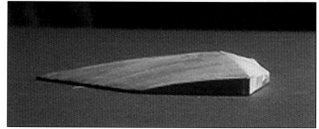

Figure 2:6

Figure 2:7

---

of the first cube. If there were, it would be perceived as floating above that cube and not behind it. Looking at this from the side (Figure 2:8) exposes what has happened. The sides have been slanted away from the light, eliminating the shadow underneath. Each piece of wood is approximately ⅜ in. thick. By leaving the top of the new cube at the same level as the top of the first cube, ⅜ in. of wood is conserved. Since the cube splits the horizon line, there is no top to carve.

Figure 2:8

Figure 2:9

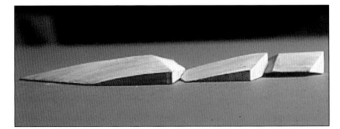

Figure 2:10

Figures 2:9 and 2:10 show how this process is continued. The difference now is that a third cube is drawn above the horizon line and the bottom is visible. The bottom surface must be carved away from the light. The natural shadow given to it by the light source is provided. It also keeps the cube visually correct in relationship to the other cubes. As you can see, an object does not necessarily need to be carved at a great depth simply because it looks farther away. Maintaining perspective along with the proper shadows contributes to the feeling of depth.

In Figure 2:11, for instance, a boat is drawn on a piece of wood. The bow of the boat appears to be farther away from your eye. In reality, it is physically closer to your eye when viewed from the top as seen in Figure 2:12. The bow is deliberately made thicker so that the extra wood is used to create richer shadows within the interior of the boat (Figure 2:13). Also, look at the way the side of the boat is slanted to the background. Once again, the tilting effect is at work. Notice that the far top edge of the boat looks as if it is curving concavely away from you. Figure 2:14 shows the carving from the top. The top edge is carved convexly, curving toward you. This was done to show how illogical relief can be. It could have been carved flat or concavely. As long as the line drawing is correct and the shadows are properly distributed, you can't pick out the discrepancy when viewing the carving from the front.

Misconceptions in Relief

False expectations about how to remove wood are common among relief carvers. Using a V tool to carve an incised line drawing is one of these misconceptions that come from how we relate to the world two-dimen-

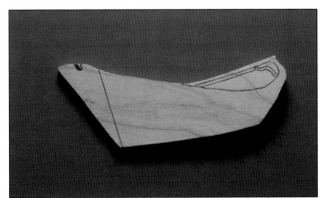

Figure 2:11

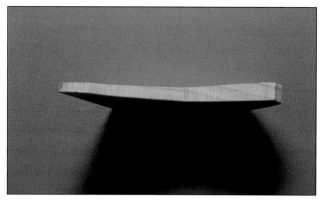

Figure 2:12

Figure 2:13

Figure 2:14

sionally. Another problem stems from the three-dimensional world. In this case, the woodcarver attempts to carve the subject in the round, using more of the thickness of the wood and increasing his chances of carving through the back, no matter how thick a piece he is working with.

Take a look at similar misconceptions with the single cube. A novice relief carver is inclined to slant the top of the cube back farther and farther, having it become more horizontal to resemble the cube as it appears in the round. What the carver fails to realize is that relief has a fixed point of view, the same as a two-dimensional painting or drawing. As your eyes move from left to right or up to down, the horizon line that helped create the image must remain constant. Slanting the top of the cube back to being horizontal may look fine when you are looking down from an oblique or to-one-side point of view; but when the view returns to being frontal, as intended, that same horizontal surface is no longer visible or visually correct.

When relief carving, do not remove any more wood than is needed to change the value of adjacent surfaces. It is the contrast that allows you to differentiate these surfaces. The angle at which the light strikes the wood is proportional to how high the relief must be. As the angle of the light source is moved more directly in front of the carving, more wood needs to be removed, and the relief will need to be higher in order to achieve enough contrast.

CHAPTER THREE

Wood and Tools

Mahogany, the Species of Choice

While there are many woods to choose from, with basswood being the number one choice for most carvers, I prefer Honduras mahogany for relief carving. Among its benefits is its dimensional stability. There is minimum expansion and contraction as seasonal humidity fluctuates. Lack of movement is particularly important because small pieces of wood can be added for a variety of components—rigging on ships, sash bars on windows, posts on houses, and even reeds or bulrushes in the compositions. If there is too much wood movement, these additions may break away, no matter how much glue is applied.

Another reason to choose mahogany is the ease with which it carves. With sharp handtools, wood slices away without a great deal of effort, and power tools reduce the wood to dust in a very short time. Patternmakers and sign carvers have recognized these qualities over the years, and they have favored mahogany over many other species.

Objects added separately, called add-ons, allow extra detail to be added to the finished shape.

Also to your advantage is mahogany's grain. While some species of wood have busy grain, which can be very distracting, mahogany's grain tends to be subdued. The goal is to have the images in the composition, not the grain of the wood, project to the viewer.

The most important reason for choosing mahogany for relief work is the color. Its reddish hue, if photographed in black and white, comes across as a neutral or middle gray. It is the perfect color when working with shadows and highlights. An equal range of value, from middle gray to black as well as middle gray to white, exists naturally. By contrast, basswood is a whiter wood. Because of its color, the range in values is reduced. While shadows are easy to achieve, highlights are not. Compare this to putting white highlights on a white piece of paper. Some carvers solve this problem by applying a darker stain in the recesses of the relief carving, a technique that enhances the contrast. The opposite is true with darker woods like walnut. It is easy to get highlights when carving it, but because the wood is so dark, it is nearly impossible to achieve contrasting shadows. Compare this to shading with a pencil on a black piece of paper. The problem with a dark wood is compounded as the wood ages and the patina continues to become even darker.

Butternut, An Alternative

Another choice for relief carving is butternut. While not as neutral as mahogany, it is close to being the same middle gray. It is also fairly easy to carve with hand and power tools, it holds details well, and it is relatively stable. However, it often has busy grain, something to avoid in relief work. To counter distracting grain with this species, choose boards, if possible, that are quartersawn to reveal simple, straight grain.

Species like cherry and oak are attractive. Unfortunately, they can be frustrating to carve because of their hardness, and they have a tendency to be very dimensionally unstable as humidity changes. A good rule of thumb is: The harder the wood, the more unstable it is. And with a wood like oak, the grain can be too strong and overpower the composition.

For the project, a piece of wood 1 ¾ in. thick is the right dimension. The thickness provides plenty of room for the five levels required plus a margin of error if a mistake is made. Relief is much more forgiving than in-the-round sculpture. If too much wood is removed on a sculpture, it is very hard to fix. With relief carving, however, the image can be simply carved in a little deeper as long as the board is thick enough.

Whatever wood you select, make sure that it is comfortable to carve, that it falls in the gray range, and that the grain won't overrule the relief carving.

Tool Choice

Many people find it odd that both power tools and handtools can work together. In relief work, these various tools have both benefits and drawbacks. Some of the operations performed in the project can be done with either power or handtools. When making your selection, consider speed or control and safety. You may find some of the power tools unwieldy and will choose to use a handtool instead. Or, handtools may be too tiring or hard to use for an extended period. It is recommended that you practice with the tools on scrap wood to gain a feel and good control before attempting to use them on the projects.

The Router

A tool common to many shops, the router is very good at removing large amounts of wood in a very short amount of time. It has the ability to establish the different levels at concise depths in a relief carving while outlining the rough shapes in the composition.

Your best choice is a plunge-type router with an easy-to-use depth adjustment. While the router provides the power, it is the bit that is doing the wood

removal. The best bit to use is a straight ½-in. bit with spiral flutes, and one made from high-speed steel is better than one made from carbide. Unlike the straight flutes of a carbide router bit, the spiral flutes clean the wood chips out of the cut with its spiral action.

While some carvers may use a V tool to do this operation, the advantages of the router include speed; but more importantly, it machine-carves at a concise 90-degree angle to the surface of the wood. It is important that each component in the composition is out-

A router is used in the beginning stages to remove large areas of wood.

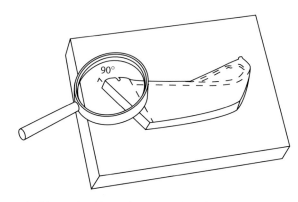

The blue and red lines demonstate how the outlined shape will get bigger or smaller as it is carved into if a 90 degree angle is not maintained when roughing out.

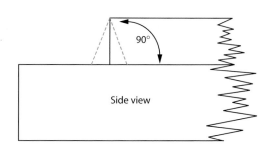

Figure 3:1

lined this way in order to maintain its precise shape as wood is removed to give it form. In this side view of a routed project (Figure 3:1) you can see how the outlined shape gets larger or smaller if it is not carved at a 90-degree angle. When this happens, the perspective of the finished carving is altered.

Controlling a router with a freehand motion can be intimidating. To help take control, make many shallow cuts rather than a single large one. Each cut should be no more than a ¼ in. deep. Get as close to the outlined area as you feel comfortable with. Any excess wood left around the outline is removed with a chisel or gouge later. Router pads work well to hold your carving in place while being routed, if the piece is not too small. Clamps or a vise should be used for smaller work.

Flexible Shaft or Micro Motor Tools

Rotary power carving tools are in essence microrouters without the worktable. They can outline shapes that are too small for their larger counterparts with remarkable speed. And, with a myriad of attachments, they have the ability to create interesting textures in the wood that can be achieved no other way.

Flexible shaft tools made by companies such as Foredom, Pfingst and others tend to have more power because of their larger motors with speeds from 14,000 to 18,000 rpm. They are workhorses that can be used for long periods of time without heating up.

Micro-motor tools like those manufactured by Dremel, RAM, NSK and others have very fast speeds up to 50,000 rpm. The higher speeds yield greater control in their use because of the number of small cuts per second they can make. A rule of thumb: The higher the rpm, the greater the control. Their small size, without having a flexible shaft attached, also contributes to the control. However, their motors are small and do not have the same ability to use larger rotary bits for removing a lot of wood quickly. They also tend to heat up with extended use. Ideally it is wise to have both kinds of rotary tools because of the different benefits offered.

With some practice, these tools can be used as if they were paintbrushes. But instead of laying on paint, the power tools lay down texture. As mentioned in the previous chapter, relief carving is similar to a monochromatic painting. The different textures that these tools make add to your palette of values.

Rotary Bits and Accessories

To carve the project with a maximum of efficiency, a list of bits and burs and their uses is provided. You will find these carving accessories available in most carving supply catalogs, woodworking stores and even hardware stores. Their uses include shaping, backcutting, sanding and texturing.

One bit in particular needs some explanation. It is referred to as the "pencil grinder," a term that will not be recognized by tool dealers, but one that will help you visualize a line-making accessory. In actuality, it is a very small and straight cylindrical bur. Look for the bit—no. 113—where Dremel accessories are sold.

The reason it is called a "pencil grinder" is that it carves a three-dimensional line—a line that has depth as well as length and width. For the project, it draws the lines that define where planes start and end. Many of

Backcutting is the removal of wood behind an object. It allows shadows to gather and gives the illusion of depth.

A pencil grinder is used to outline each area and establish a depth for that plane.

Step-by-Step Relief Carving

the cuts you will be making are tapering cuts. This means that the cut will go into the line at a specific depth and then progressively get deeper to its end. Depths are supplied in the project's picture captions as applicable. They are meant to be a general guide. If the cut becomes a "little" deeper, there is no need to worry. The relief becomes just a little deeper. Remember that relief is a very forgiving art form in that respect. The depth of the cut is measured by inserting the tip of the bit into the cut, then placing your finger at the top of the cut. Remove the bit from the cut and measure the distance from the tip to the finger.

Using the pencil grinder well can be tricky. Practice trying to make straight cuts in a piece of scrap wood until you feel comfortable with its control. You will find it easier to make these cuts in multiple passes, going over the same line many times until the proper depth is achieved. Keep the sawdust out of the cut since it will obstruct your vision of what is actually happening. Make the cuts 90 degrees to the surface of the wood. Remember how this controls the true outline shape in the drawing (Figure 3:1).

One other accessory you will be using is a miniature table saw made by combining a block of hardwood and a

flexible shaft handpiece. The saw is used for cutting out small pieces of wood veneer, a process that is too dangerous on a standard-size table saw. It is fairly simple to make. The details of its design are described in Figure 3:2.

Rotary Tools for the Project
- Pencil grinder bit (Dremel no. 113) – cutting in
- Inverted cone-shaped bur (Foredom no. P3) – detailing
- Ball-shaped cutters: 2mm, 4mm, 5mm – texturing water
- ½-in. conical aluminum oxide stone – texturing and smoothing
- ½-in. cylindrical aluminum oxide stone – sanding
- ¼-in. rotary steel wire brush – texturing
- ½-in. Scotch-Brite™ disk and mandrel – smoothing
- ⅛-in. helix drill bit – back-cutting
- 1-in. disk-shaped carbide bur – backcutting
- Conical carbide bur – back-slanting
- Miniature tablesaw

Edge and other Handtools

When you want to make clean controlled cuts, edge tools such as chisels, gouges and knives become essential. While cuts with these tools are more time consuming to make than with power tools, the slower pace allows for more critical thinking as the project progresses. The dust and noise created by power carving can be very distracting, not only to your demeanor but also to your critical eye.

Chisels, which are the flat tools, work best on convex surfaces. They produce the smoothest result in this situation since the corners of the edge do not dig in and do not produce as high of a scallop between each adjacent cut as a gouge does (see Figure 3:3).

Gouges work well on flat and concave surfaces. In most cases, do not use a gouge deeper than a no. 3. The reason for this is that a deeper gouge is used more for roughing out where larger amounts of wood need to be removed. If you use a router, most of the waste wood is removed quickly and efficiently, eliminating the need for deeper gouges. Also be aware that shallower gouges create less of a scallop between their adjacent cuts (see Figure 3:4). The deeper the gouge, the higher the scal-

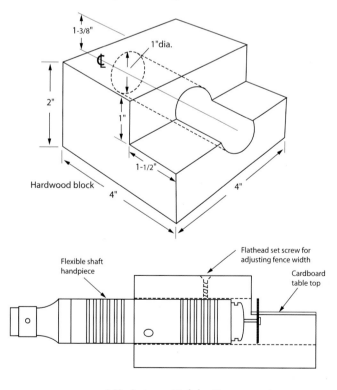

Miniature Table Saw

Figure 3:2

lop. If these scallops become too high, they have a tendency to fool your eyes in how they perceive the shapes progressing.

Because the nature of relief carving requires working in hollows, a knife does not work well for removing a lot of wood. However, it does come in handy for carving fine details where the cutting angle allows it. A hobby knife with a very thin blade does not crush the wood fibers as it cuts, and the problems of splitting and chipping out the wood are reduced. In other places you will find that a knife with a more durable, thicker blade works well for cutting in lines for stop cuts or creating fine shadows.

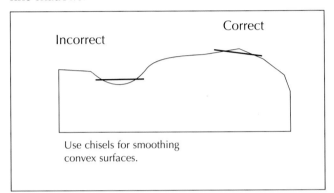

Use chisels for smoothing convex surfaces.

Figure 3:3

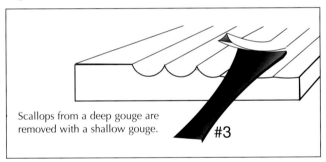

Scallops from a deep gouge are removed with a shallow gouge. #3

Figure 3:4

Handtools are ideal for a number of tasks, including wood removal, detailing and finishing.

V tools are two chisels joined together by one edge to make a V shape. Three typical angles are 45, 60 and 90 degrees, but others exist. They are useful for cleaning corners where two adjacent planes come together.

Rifflers are rasps that are typically double-ended with a handle in between. The ends can be straight, curved, flat, triangular, convex or knife-like. While they are excellent for getting into areas that are inaccessible to most carving tools, a riffler, especially one with a medium cut, will smooth a flat surface more easily and cleanly than sandpaper.

Handtools for the Project

- ¼-in. chisel
- 1-in. chisel
- No. 3 ⅜-in. gouge
- No. 3 ¾-in. gouge
- 70-degree ¼-in. V tool
- Hobby knife
- Carving knife
- Flat-bent riffler

An Ideal Workbench

As discussed earlier, creating a relief carving is not unlike painting a two-dimensional portrait or scene. If you ever watch a painter at work, you notice he uses an easel so that he can step back from the canvas and give it his critical eye. The near vertical orientation is obvious. The same needs hold true for the relief carver.

A workbench that can be elevated to an 80-degree angle will act as your easel. The top should be con-

A nearly vertical workbench allows light to strike the work in progress at the correct angle.

structed from 2-in.-thick hardwood so that steel hold-downs can be used to secure the carving to the workbench. The heavy top also allows for mallet work if a project calls for it. This steep working angle is easy on your back and allows woodchips to fall away from the carving as you make them.

If you decide to use a flexible shaft tool, you should make an allowance for the motor to be hung in a convenient place. It needs to be readily accessible and the shaft should not have to bend at a tight angle when being used.

Lighting

Lighting is one of the most important aspects of your workspace. An incandescent light should be placed above the carving workbench so that it shines down across the work surface at a slight angle. Fluorescent lights are not recommended because they are too diffused. A photographer's lighting fixture, which can accept a high-wattage bulb—200 watts is preferable for this kind of relief work—can be purchased at most camera shops. An alternative is a swing-arm lamp that is adjustable and can be attached directly to the side of your workbench.

The light you select is going to provide the single source by which all of the surfaces of the carving are defined. With that in mind, it is important that the workroom not be naturally bright. If there are windows, draw the shades. If there are other electric lights, turn them off. Indirect light creeping into the work area makes highlights and shadows less noticeable. And make sure to keep the light source in one place. Moving it around will confuse your eyes.

Pattern and Adhesives

Included are two types of patterns for the project. One is a simple line drawing that provides the general outline of each component in the composition as well as the depths of the cuts. Make a copy of this for routing the wood and an extra copy to use as a guide. The other drawing includes the fine details, textures and values of the scene. Make five copies of this drawing to be cut up and applied as the carving progresses.

Spray adhesives work well for applying these drawings to the wood. 3M's Super 77 spray adhesive works

well for the routing stage where you don't want the drawing to peel off. In the later stages of the project, it is beneficial to be able to easily remove the paper drawing. A replaceable, photo-mount type of spray adhesive is recommended. Both types of adhesives are available at office supply stores.

Yellow wood glue is a good adhesive to have around for general mishaps. In addition, you will need glue to apply the final details. Comprising small pieces of wood and veneer, these details are simply too small, or their grain orientation is wrong, to be carved in place. They will most likely break off during the subtractive part of the project.

Levels should be clearly marked before beginning to remove wood.

CHAPTER FOUR

Exercises in Perspective and Illusion

The following exercises are designed to actually let you experience the concepts of perspective and illusion. The blocks illustrated in Chapter 2 demonstrate that the human eye can be fooled by the proper use of perspective. Carving them is a good exercise in creating a composition with multiple components—one set behind another—that shows how relief is done without literally cutting through the back of the board. You will see for yourself how the surfaces of the wood are manipulated to change their color values. The exercises will help build confidence and reduce the anxiety that is often associated with removing wood. Make sure your work light is above and to the left or right of the project. It will help you see the different values in the wood as it is carved.

An Exercise in Perspective

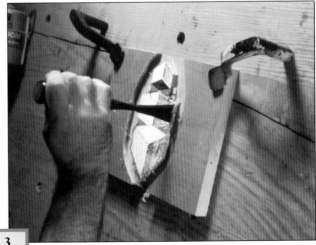

1 This piece incorporates two vanishing points to show how the lines relate). Study the drawing. If the box is below the horizon line, the top of the box is visible. If the box splits the horizon line, the top and the bottom of the box aren't visible at all. Above the horizon line, the bottom of the box is visible.

2 Remove wood from around the boxes with a router to a depth of ⅜ in. Stay as close to the edge as you feel comfortable.

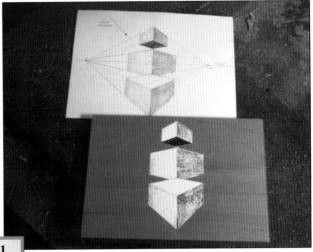

3 Clean up the outlines with a chisel. Make sure these cuts remain 90 degrees to the surface of the background.

Cube Exercise Pattern

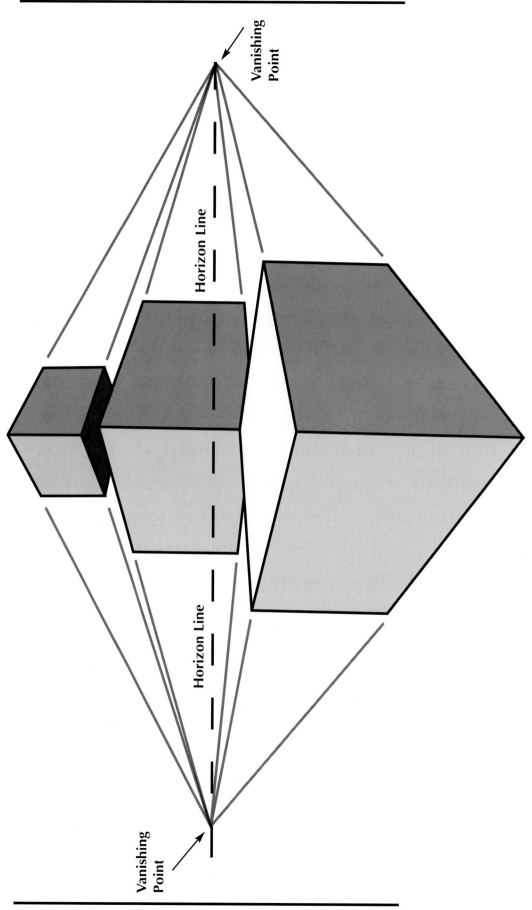

Vanishing Point

Horizon Line

Horizon Line

Vanishing Point

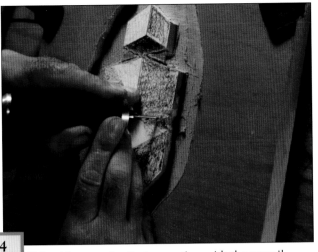

5 The roughed-in blocks are ready to be carved. The result is different values associated with the individual planes.

4 Take this opportunity to practice with the pencil grinder and use it in the tight corners where the router cannot reach. The tool is very much like a router, but it works on a smaller scale, removing wood from small areas that big routers can't reach. Outlining the box with the pencil grinder makes a stop cut. The rest of the wood is removed with a chisel.

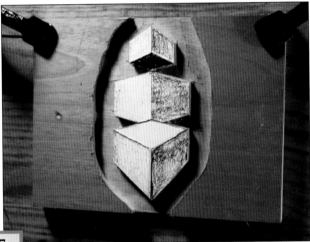

6 First, make a tapering cut with the pencil grinder. The line tapers to ⅜ in. deep at the bottom to meet the background wood.

7 The finished pencil grinder cut looks like this. The cut keeps defining where this line is as the wood is progressively carved away.

8 Make cuts with the pencil grinder to define each line in the piece. Perspective will dictate the depth of each line.

9 Carve the right side of the bottom box with a no. 3 ⅝-in. gouge. Keep in mind that you are simply connecting lines with a plane. The plane tapers to match the depth of the pencil grinder cuts.

10 The roughed-in plane looks like this. Notice how the shadow that was once under the cube is now transferred to its side and the wood becomes darker.

11 Flatten the side of the cube with a 1-in. chisel. Make sure to create a crisp corner where the bottom of the cube meets the background. Do not leave any shadow under the cube.

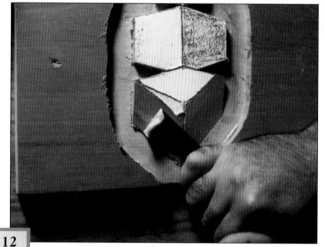

13 The top is slanted back so that it reflects the light to make it whiter. All the pencil cuts have been eliminated; all surfaces of the cube are defined by a value or contrast instead of a line.

12 Remove wood from the other side of the cube with the chisel.

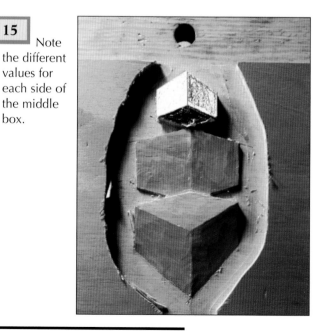

15 Note the different values for each side of the middle box.

14 Carve the middle block. Taper the sides back and slant them down. Tapering eliminates the shadow cast on the top of the lower box. Because this block is viewed head on, only the two sides are seen.

Step-by-Step Relief Carving

16 Angle the sides back for the top block. This time, however, do not slant the sides down as you did before.

17 Tilt the bottom of the cube back to create a dark value.

18 The excess wood is removed to show a side view of the carving. Notice that visually, from the front, the cubes look to be positioned behind or above one another. However, as you can see from the side, all of the cubes are on the same plane. The illusion of perspective is one of the secrets behind successful relief carving.

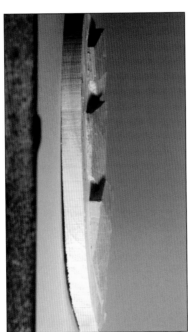

19 Experiment and practice by creating other cubes within cubes and connecting lines with planes.

An Exercise in Illusion

Many beginning relief carvers feel that the farther away an image looks in the composition, the deeper it needs to be carved. Carving an egg on a shelf illustrates the difference between physical and visual space. Here the egg is physically closer to your eye when looked at from the front, being one of the highest parts in the relief (see step 10), yet visually it appears to be farther away than the front edge of the shelf. Try this last exercise in relief carving before moving on to the project.

1 First, roughly outline the egg with a router and then a 1-in. chisel.

Egg Exercise Pattern

2   Next, remove wood from the bottom of the board to form the top of the shelf.

3   Remove wood from the top of the board to form the wall behind the shelf. The wall is tilted in toward the middle of the carving to give it a darker value than the top of the shelf.

4   Carefully smooth out the surfaces using a gouge. The surfaces do not have to be as perfectly flat as you might think. The straight lines associated with the front edge of the shelf make your brain think it is flat.

5   A view from the side shows the different levels of the carving as well as how the seemingly flat shelf surface is actually curved.

6   Now begin to shape the egg. Start at the outside of the oval and work your way toward the center.

7   Shape the top of the egg last, removing very little wood at the top center point. Round the egg over toward the edges and undercut it with a pencil grinder.

Step-by-Step Relief Carving

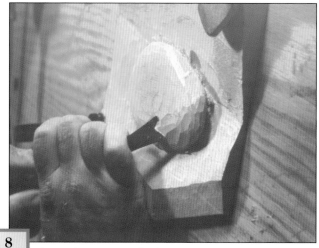

8 The undercut is made deeper and more prominent with the 1-in. chisel.

9 The finished egg lies on the edge of the shelf.

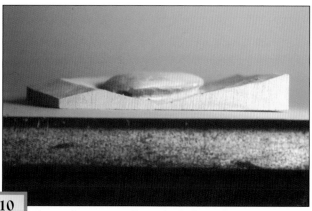

10 The undercutting allows for light to flow behind the egg. The other illusion to note is the background wall. It is the highest part of the relief and physically it is the closest to your eyes. However, when viewed from the front, the wall is visually farther away than any other component in the composition.

CHAPTER FIVE

The Project

This project is intended to allow the carver to practice the theory mentioned in the prior text and exercises. It will illustrate how each component in the theory can work together to create an entire composition in relief. Referring to the prior chapters will better help you understand the concepts in this project.

Carving for Safety's Sake

Safety should be everyone's concern. Here are ten tips to keep in mind when using tools and wood to make a woodcarving:

1. Keep your tools sharp.
2. When making dust or using chemicals, cover up the nose and mouth. When making noise, cover up the ears.
3. Dispose of rags that have been used to apply oil finishes in water-filled metal or plastic containers.
4. Don't carve when you are tired or distracted.
5. Read the instructions that come with power tools.
6. Protect your hands.
7. Make yourself comfortable.
8. Wear goggles or a face shield when power sharpening or carving.
9. Make sure your carving is securely clamped or held down.
10. When in doubt about carving tools and techniques, take lessons from the experts.

© David Bennett

Boat Illustration Pattern

Getting Started

1 The project pattern includes two types of drawings. You are going to use the simple line drawing first for the routing stage. The simple outline is less confusing to the eye when you are trying to see the edges of each component in the composition. The extra half inch of wood on both sides of the drawing is provided for clamping purposes. You may notice some details missing in this drawing. They are added later.

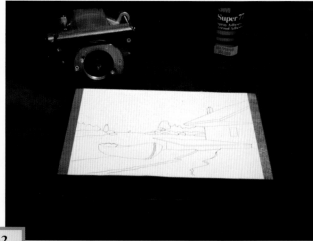

2 Using permanent spray adhesive—3M's Super 77 works well—spray the back of the pattern and attach it directly to the wood. It is important to use a permanent, non-removable adhesive. You will be using a router in a later step to remove wood, and you do not want the router base lifting the pattern.

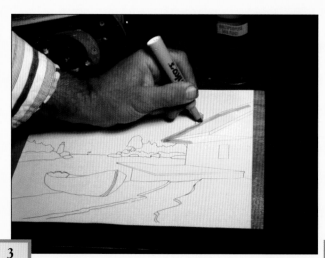

3 Creating levels is one of the hardest concepts for beginners to grasp. To facilitate the process, use a different colored marker to show each level. The white of the paper is on the highest level, which includes the boat and the foreground. Blue shows the second level: the house, the shallow water and the top cloud, which are drawn in later.

4 Yellow marks the third level. This includes the water in the mid-ground of the illustration and the middle cloud, which are drawn later.

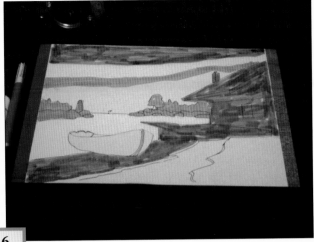

5 The fourth level is colored red. It includes the islands in the distance and the bottom cloud. The middle cloud (yellow, level two) and the top cloud (blue, level one) have been colored.

DEPTH MEASUREMENTS BY LEVEL

Level	Subject	Depth
Level 1 (White)	boat	0″
	foreground	0″
Level 2 (Blue)	house	1/4″
	shallow water	1/4″
Level 3 (Yellow)	water	1/2″
	top cloud	1/2″
Level 4 (Red)	islands	3/4″
	middle cloud	3/4″
Level 5 (Purple)	bottom cloud	1″
Level 6 (Gray)	sky	1 1/8″

Tip: A piece of carpet padding placed under the carving keeps the wood from sliding around while routing is taking place. Make sure that the pad is larger than the surface of the project.

6 The fifth level encompasses only one item: the farthest reaches of the sky. If you are still having trouble visualizing the different levels of this pattern, imagine that you can reach into the drawing, all the way to the back of the scene. In what order would your hand pass the objects as you reached across to the sky? The bank is in the foreground, then the boat. Next comes the house, the shallow water just beyond the boat and the cloud at the top of the picture. Then you pass the deeper water in the center of the scene and the middle cloud. The islands and the far-away cloud are the last objects you pass before your hand reaches into the sky at the back of the illustration.

Roughing Cut

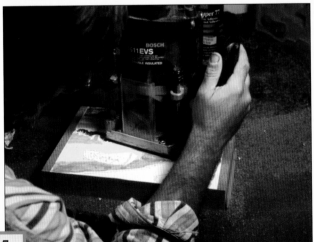

7 Start removing wood from level 5, the deepest level, a process that leaves a platform for the base of the router. A plunge router with a ½-in.-diameter straight spiral-fluted router bit is recommended. A spiral bit is ideal because it pulls the wood chips out of the cut. Bits that are not spiral leave chips in the cut. These chips can get hot as the bit rotates and may cause a fire or singe the wood.

8 Remove wood in ¼-in. increments to a depth of 1⅛ in. Be sure to remove only small amounts of wood at a time and to stay ⅛ in. away from the edges. That distance gives you a margin of error and is removed later.

9 When you are finished removing wood from the deepest level, take a look at your work. You will notice that the router leaves ragged paper behind, which makes it difficult to see the edges of the levels. To remedy this, carefully clear away the paper with a hobby knife.

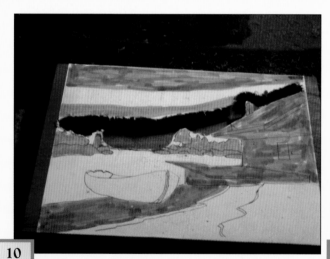

10 The wood is removed from Level 5 and the torn edges of the pattern are trimmed. You are now ready to move on to the next level.

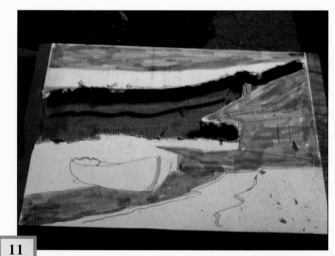

11 Remove all of the red-colored areas of Level 4. Notice that the section for the islands is reduced to a different depth than the section that becomes the bottom cloud. The islands are ¾ in. deep; the bottom cloud is 1 in. deep.

12 Make sure that the routing leaves all of the levels at their correct depths.

13 Relief carving is very similar to painting. By removing wood, you are essentially painting a picture with light and shadows. An angled easel or work surface allows you to step back from your work, and it is more comfortable on your back. Clamp the work to the easel. Steel holddowns will clamp the project quickly. Striking a holddown with a mallet tightens it. Striking it from underneath the bench loosens it.

14 Notice how the light, which is directly above the easel, creates shadows and contrast on the carving. If you flood the piece with light from all angles, there are no shadows and, subsequently, no contrast. Keep in mind that in relief carving you are working somewhere between the second and third dimension. Flat art that includes paintings is two-dimensional; sculpture is three-dimensional.

15 Take a second copy of the simple line drawing and cut out each component with a hobby knife.
The paper pieces lie flat on the shapes created by the router.

Step-by-Step Relief Carving

16 Use permanent spray adhesive to glue components of the pattern to the levels. Work begins on the house, the boat and the islands. Note that the routed wooden shapes are larger than the pattern pieces because of the ⅛-in. margin of error left during the routing process.

17 Refine the outlines of the levels with a pencil grinder.

18 Run the pencil grinder along the outlines and to the bottom of each adjacent level. Outlining must be done with as much accuracy as possible. Mark the end of the bit with a magic marker or judge the correct depth by eye. Don't go below the established level, which will cause too much wood to be removed.

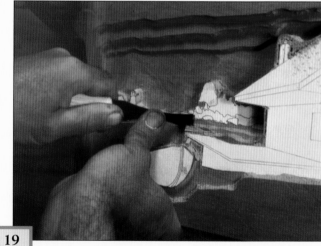

19 Chisels and gouges can also be used to refine the outlines, but take extra care when working with end grain. Using handtools in these areas may cause the wood to splinter. You will find the pencil grinder is preferable when making stop cuts in end grain.

Building Form

20 You can also use the pencil grinder to outline a small area and then pop out the wood with a gouge.

21 When you are ready to start the actual relief carving, begin with the areas closest to you. Work from the outside in. Make a cut with the pencil grinder to define the line that marks where the soffit meets the wall. The area is an "inside corner" that appears where one plane meets another. The line is a tapering cut: ⅛ in. deep on the right and ⅜ in. deep on the left. The depth of the line reflects how deep the relief carving should be.

22 Continue defining the edges of the house with the pencil grinder. The side and facia lines require non-tapering cuts, ⅛ in. deep. The line where the wall stops and the porch begins is a tapering line: ⅛ in. deep on the right to ⅜ in. deep on the left.

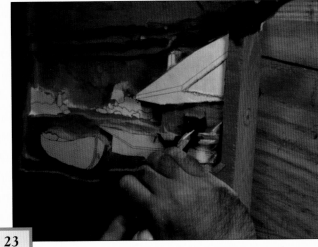

23 The beginning stages of relief carving require that you simply connect lines with planes. Connect, for example, the line that marks the bottom of the wall and the line that marks the top of the wall with a plane. Using a 1-in. chisel, work from the bottom of the piece to the top. The plane (or wall) will taper from ⅛ in. at the "front" to ⅜ in. deep at the "back." Try to match the depth of the line that you cut in steps 21 and 22 with the pencil grinder.

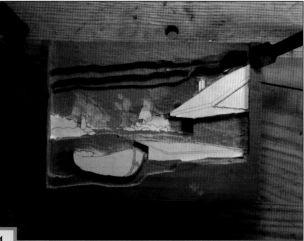

24 The wall of the house is complete. Note that the line from the pencil grinder is no longer visible. It is important to completely remove this line. Lines are not a part of nature; and if you do not remove the line, your carving will appear unnatural. A "virtual line" forms naturally if the connected planes have different values.

25 Use the no. 3 ¾-in. gouge to form "outside corners." Here, the soffit is being carved. Notice the shade of the wood under the soffit. It appears much darker than the wall because its surface is tilted away from the light.

26 Continue to shape the soffit with the no. 3 ¾-in. gouge. The gable is carved in the same way by connecting the pencil cuts with a plane. Notice the corner where the wall and soffit meet. It should resemble a folded-in piece of paper, and there must be no remnant left of the pencil cut.

27 Use a 70-degree ¼-in. V tool to create the slight shadow where the fascia is set away from the wall. Be sure to use the V tool to completely remove the line left by the pencil grinder.

28 Use the no. 3 ¾ in. gouge to carve the roof back, tilting it toward the light so that its value is lighter than the adjacent fascia. Do not slant it more than ¼ in. It is easy to be fooled here because it may seem logical to slope the roof as it looks in real life. Relief can be very counter-intuitive.

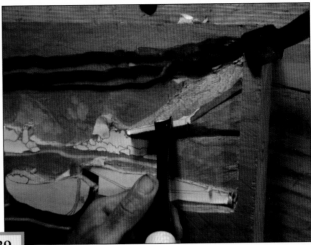

29 The roof creates another plane. Be careful not to remove the slight edge where the base of the roof meets the fascia.

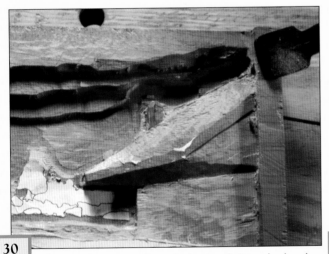

30 Take a minute to make a "value study." Look closely at the house. Notice all the different light and dark values that allow you to see the various surfaces of the house. The strong light shining from above creates shadows that allow your eye to distinguish between the roof, the fascia, the soffit, the wall and the peak. The basic shape of the house is taking form with no more than ⅜ in. of wood removed.

31 Use the no. 3 ¾-in. gouge to slope the porch surface back to the wall of the house. Once again, the corner where the two surfaces meet should resemble a fold-in piece of paper, and there should be no remnant of the pencil grinder line. Notice how the surface of the porch is a lighter value than the wall.

The Project

32 Create the overhang of the porch where it meets the stone foundation by outlining it with the pencil grinder about ⅛ in. deep. Do the same where the foundation meets the wall. Once these stop cuts are made, the surface of the stone foundation is carved using the 70-degree ¼-in. V tool. Remember to slope the left side of the foundation back about ¼ in. to create its corner as seen in Step 33.

33 Create the ground and shoreline by connecting the levels. Use the no. 3 ¾-in. gouge to taper the foreground from the edge of the carving into the stone wall of the porch.

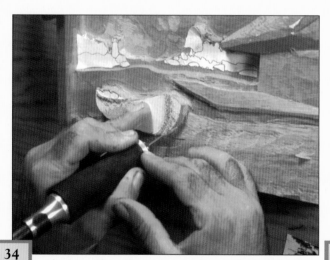

34 Cut the inside corners that form the bow of the boat with the pencil grinder. This is a tapering line, starting at 1/16 in. deep at the top of the boat and ending level with the ground.

35 Still using the pencil grinder, cut a line ¼ in. deep across the top of the boat.

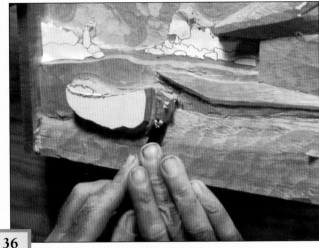

36 Start to shape the hull of the boat. Use the no. 3 ⁵⁄₈-in. gouge to remove wood from the right side of the bow. Round this area sparingly by removing no more than ⅛ in. of wood. It is backcut later to allow light to flow behind it.

37 Shape the left side of the boat and remove wood from the interior with the no. 3 ⁵⁄₈-in. gouge. Notice the way the shadow from under the boat in the previous photo is transferred to the side of the hull, which gives the hull the appearance of being rounded.

38 After the boat is shaped, connect the shoreline in the foreground to the islands and horizon line to form the surface of the water. A tapering pencil cut under the islands acts as a stop cut.

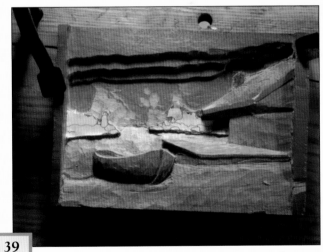

39 Do another value check before moving on to the next section. The top of the boat should be highlighted; the bottom of the boat should recede into shadow. Also notice how the water to the left of the boat is slightly shadowed when compared to the water at the horizon.

40 Use the pencil grinder to outline the top of the islands about ¼ in. deep. This stop cut aids in tapering the sky to meet the water.

41 Create another tapering stop cut with the pencil grinder to connect all of the routed levels of the sky to the horizon line. This stop cut links up with the stop cut made in the previous step.

42 Use the no. 3 ¾-in. gouge to remove the steps in the sky. In this step, all of the pencil cuts are connected with a curving plane.

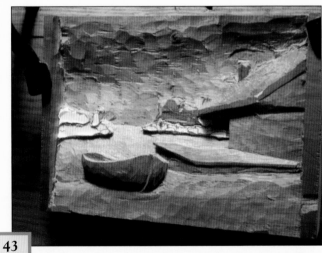

43 When you have finished carving the sky, do another value check. Observe how curving the sky gives it a gradient value that is darker at the top and lighter at the horizon line. The water is the lightest value. Now make tapering pencil cuts where the foliage meets the rocks of the islands as seen on the left. After the pencil cuts are made, use the no. 3 ¾-in. gouge to tilt the surfaces of the foliage and rocks to meet at the bottom of the pencil cut as seen on the island at the right.

44 As you continue, keep the shaded drawing close to your work. A quick study of the drawing will answer many questions you may have about perspective.

45 Use a ¼-in. chisel to shape the trees of the island behind the house. Note that the trunks of the trees are recessed farther back than the tops of the trees. General shapes are all that is needed.

46 Define the surfaces of the rocks with a series of V cuts using the 70-degree ¼-in. V tool. Do not use it to outline the rocks. If you look closely, the surfaces are created in a zigzag fashion with two values. The sides of the rocks are dark and their tops are light. Merely outlining the rocks will detract from their three-dimensional appearance.

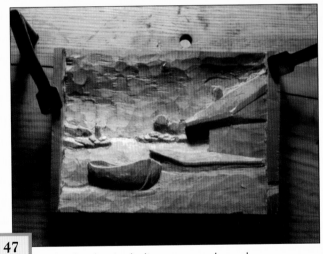

47 Both islands—including trees, rocks and lighthouse—are rough-carved. Notice that all of the undercuts are carved away when shaping the rocks.

Backcutting

48 Now that all of the general shapes have been formed correctly, you can begin the process of backcutting, which removes wood behind a feature to eliminate unnatural shadows. Do not do any backcutting until all the areas of your carving are roughed in. This process is left until now so that if mistakes are made in forming, they can be fixed by carving in a little deeper. Use the following tools (left to right): a conical carbide bur, a disk-shaped carbide bur, and a ⅛-in. helix drill bit.

49 Begin by using the helix drill bit to backcut the roof.

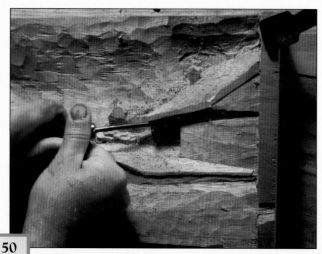

50 Backcut the soffit as well. Note that backcutting is different from undercutting, which involves making a deeper cut to create a heavier shadow or a greater highlight.

51 Backcut the chimney.

TIP: When using the drill to backcut, start by nosing the point into the wood. A side-to-side motion allows the flutes to cut. Drill bits with high helix-type flutes (available at industrial supply houses) have a raised edge on each flute and cut aggressively with more control. Practice on scrap wood before attempting it on your project.

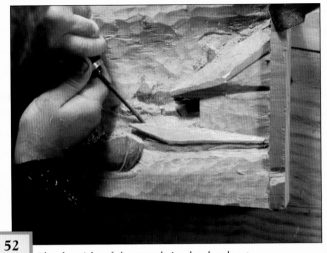

52 The far side of the porch is also backcut.

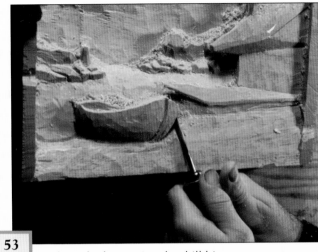

53 Backcut the boat using the drill bit.

54 A disk-shaped carbide bur in the flexible shaft tool speeds up wood removal behind the boat.

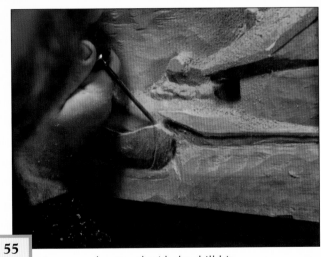

55 More wood removal with the drill bit.

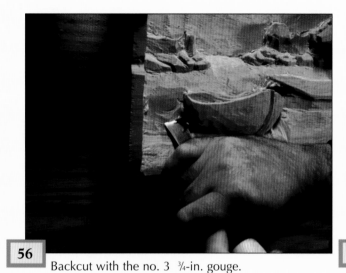

56 Backcut with the no. 3 ¾-in. gouge.

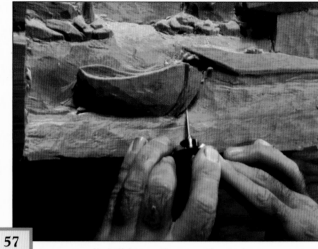

57 Use a small drill bit or the pencil grinder to remove wood from behind the bow.

58 Backcut the porch overhang to remove wood from under the porch.

59 Use a no. 3 ⅜-in. gouge to carve away the horizontal surfaces left by the router. Slant them back so that they are no longer visible when viewing the carving from the front. When doing this, it is good to remember that tall and short people will be viewing the carving and each will have his own unique viewing angle.

60 Put a back-slant on the back edge of the roof.

61 Create a back-slant on the back vertical edge of the house.

62 Use the pencil grinder to provide a back-slant to the edges of the chimney. A power tool is preferable in this area because of the way the grain is oriented.

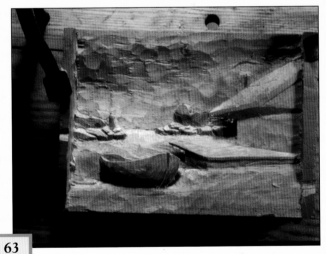

63 Make another check of the carving at this point. Make sure that all the backcutting is complete. Notice how the light flows behind the surfaces that were backcut.

Detailing

64   Now you are ready to detail the surfaces. Take a photocopy of the shaded drawing and cut it into pieces to fit the surfaces of the carving. At this point, you will see how closely the carving is conforming to the drawing. The objective is to use the drawing as a template for locating the details. The nuances of perspective are already in place on the paper. Drawing them onto the wood freehand can be very counter-intuitive. Don't worry about the water or background just yet—these details are created with texture later on.

65   Use a removable photo mount or spray adhesive to tack down each piece of paper. Be sure to spray only the paper. On flat surfaces, like those shown here, the paper fits easily. You may find it necessary to trim the drawing depending on how well the beginning stages are carved.

66   Since the surface of the boat is now curved, you will find that the straight piece of paper is too short. Split the difference between the two ends of the hull.

67   Trace the lines on the paper with a carving knife. Use the tool to carve the lines that form the board-and-batten-style vertical siding. The goal is to create visible lines, so don't use a knife with a very thin blade. Note that the lines of the roof are cut in and the paper is removed.

68 Continue to "knife in" the lines on the walls of the house.

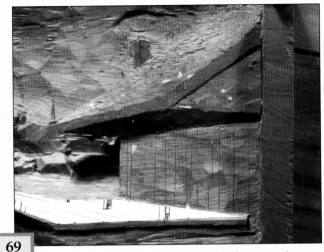

69 Remove the paper pattern carefully. If you used removable adhesive to tack the paper to the wood, it should come up easily with just a slight pull. Check to make sure all the line are visible and go over the ones that are not.

70 Use the ¼-in. chisel to carve the flat surfaces of the shingles. Think of each course or row of shingles as a tapering cut that connects one line to another. Do not simply cut the lines in with a V tool. Use a knife to add the lines that run down the roof. These lines, also known as "rain marks," must run parallel to the gable line or edge of the roof. Start cutting in the rain marks at one edge or the other, working toward the middle and finishing at the opposite end.

71 Create the shapes of the stones in the chimney with a small inverted cone-shaped bur.

72 Use the pencil grinder to create the recesses of the battens in the siding.

73 A note on perspective: Siding lines become narrower and closer together as they recede into the background. Less contrast is needed on elements that are farther away from the viewer. Use the pencil grinder to carve the larger, deeper lines toward the front of the house; use the inverted cone-shaped bur for the smaller, shallower lines toward the back of the house. Note that the lines stop at the areas where the window and door are located.

74 Use the pencil grinder to outline the sections of the window. Pop out the pieces with the chisel. In order to create a shadow here, the window must be deeply recessed.

75 The hole created by carving in the window has four flat sides and a bottom. Backcut the four sides to eliminate any light reflecting from them. If not removed, they may appear to look like an interior wall or floor, something that your eyes will find illogical. Carve the door by slightly recessing it.

76 Use the inverted cone-shaped bur to add details to the door. Add lines to show the vertical, horizontal and diagonal wooden planks of the door.

77 With the knife, which must be extra sharp, cut through the paper pattern to create the lines of the deck planking on the top of the porch. The lines should be deep and dark enough so that they are visible. Be sure to use the knife and not a V tool for these details. The V tool makes a line that is unnaturally wide for this area.

78 Use the corner of the pencil grinder as if it were a V tool to carry the lines of the deck planking over onto the front edge of the porch. Work the edges of the deck planks to make it appear that they have thickness.

79 Define the stones in the stone wall of the porch with the inverted cone-shaped bur.

80 Carve the faces of the stones with the knife. Strive to give each stone dimension. Remember, there are no lines in nature.

81 A ½-in. conical aluminum oxide stone smoothes and adds dimension to the stones.

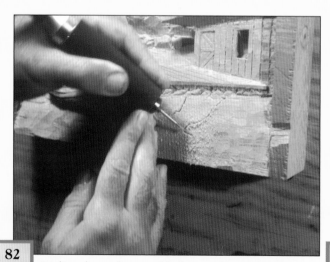

82 Outline the pathway with the pencil grinder. The cuts need to be ⅛ in. deep. Note how the lines start far apart and end closer together to maintain perspective.

83 Carve the pathway with the no. 3 ⅝-in. gouge.

84 Cut in the lines to show the planking on the sides of the boat.

85 Remove the paper pattern and use a ¼-in. chisel to undercut the planks on the boat. Strive for the same saw-tooth pattern that was created on the shingles.

86 Slightly slant the top surface of the transom, where the outboard motor is mounted, to give it the appearance of thickness.

87 Use a flat-bent riffler to smooth out any chisel marks. Sandpaper is not recommended because it rounds the edges of the carving, and clarity is lost.

88 Begin to texture the water. Divide the water into four sections with a pencil. Each section becomes progressively smaller as you move toward the horizon. Three different sizes of ball cutters and the small inverted cone are needed to texture each of these sections, which get progressively smaller.

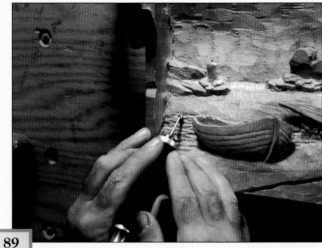

89 Use a 5mm ball-shaped cutter to texture to the water closest to the shore. Make long elliptical cuts parallel to the horizon line. Since this part of the water is closest to your eye, these cuts will be the darkest and in turn the deepest—approximately ½ in. long by ¹⁄₁₆ in. deep—for the water texture. The goal is to texture the surface of the water to give it the appearance of waves.

90 As you move back to the next section, use a 3mm ball carver and make shorter, shallower cuts. A 2mm ball cutter is used for the next section. The transition from larger cuts to smaller cuts should appear seamless.

91 The inverted cone is used to make the shortest and shallowest cuts in the section at the horizon. Perspective is important here. All of the cuts for the waves, including those made at the horizon, must run parallel to the bottom of the carving.

TIP: When working with the ball cutters, do not use the very tips because that is where all of the cutting flutes come together and become very shallow. It is more efficient to use the parts of the cutters where the flutes are deepest.

92 Use a ¾-in. rotary wire brush to remove "fuzzies" or raised grain. Keep in mind that the brush cuts quickly and eliminates texture if you push too hard. Dust can be a problem when using power tools; wear eye protection and a dust mask.

93 Use the wire brush to texture the ground and the grass.

94 Clean up the raised grain on other areas of the carving with the wire brush.

95 Use the pencil grinder to add texture to the foliage on the islands. The darkest part of a forest is on the bottom where the light can't penetrate; you need to add the most texture where the foliage meets the island.

96 Carve deep, randomly shaped holes in the trees to simulate foliage with the pencil grinder. The depth at which these holes are carved controls their value. The deeper the holes, the darker the value. Take care not to create perfectly round cavities, which tend to look like unnatural "wormholes" instead of foliage.

97 Make the surface of the foliage appear to undulate by varying the depth of the cuts. Try not to create a pattern of similar shapes and sizes. It detracts from a natural look to the trees. The inverted cone-shaped bur can be used to add an even finer texture.

98 Do a value check on the foliage before you begin to clean up the area. The area where the trees meet the ground should appear to be recessed and dark.

99 Use the wire brush to backcut the foliage and to allow light to shine behind the island. Do not backcut the lighthouse at this time. It should be left connected so that it is stable when you cut in the detail in the next steps.

100 Detail the lighthouse with the pencil grinder. Do not use a chisel to add details; the lighthouse is too small and may crack or break.

101 When the lighthouse is detailed, backcut it with the gouge or the wire brush and the pencil grinder.

102 Make a series of V cuts with the no. 3 ¾-in. gouge to enhance the perspective of the clouds. Use the same saw-tooth pattern that was used on the shingles and on the boat. When you look at a cloud in the sky, you see only the bottom and the face of the cloud.

103 The basic forms of the clouds are now set in. Do a quick value check to make sure that only two values are apparent: dark for the underside and white for the cloud face. The clouds at the top of the carving are bigger; those closer to the horizon are smaller.

104 Use the no. 3 ¾-in. gouge to break the basic shapes into smaller shapes. Avoid creating a repeating pattern. Patterns are found in man-made structures such as brick walls; nature creates random shapes, sizes and textures.

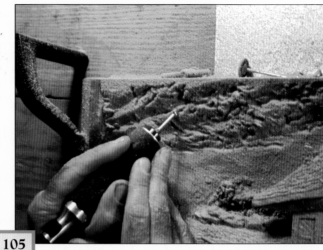

105 When the general shaping is done, round hard edges left by the gouge with the 5mm ball cutter. The bit also adds smaller shadows to the clouds and further enhances their forms.

106 The rotary wire brush is used to texture and round the surfaces of the clouds.

107 Use 3mm and 2mm ball cutters on the clouds that recede into the background.

108 Alternate between the ball cutters and the rotary wire brush to create the final texture.

109 Use the face of a ½-in. cylindrical aluminum oxide stone to sand and smooth the clear part of the sky.

110 Continue to smooth the clear part of the sky by following the stone with the rotary wire brush.

111 Use Scotch-Brite™ mounted on a mandrel to sand and de-burr the carving.

Adding in Final Details

112 Many of the final details—porch posts, dock posts, shutters, sash bars and bulrushes—are added separately because they are too fragile to carve. Start by cutting a piece of wood for the porch posts. Once again, use the drawing as a template to make sure the pieces are properly proportioned.

113 The post is carved from a square piece of wood. Carve off the back to make a thin triangular shape. Two surfaces of the shape are used to simulate the two visible surfaces of the porch post that are seen in the drawing. Make the post longer than is needed so it will properly fit later.

114 Use the pencil grinder to make a small hole in the soffit for the top of the post. Wood expands and contracts according to the seasonal changes in humidity. If both ends of the post are glued to the carving, the piece will pop off as the wood changes dimensionally. Therefore, only one end is glued.

115 Insert the post and cut it to length.

116 Fit the top end of the post into the hole. Once the top is fit in, the bottom of the post is trimmed off at an angle so that it sits on the porch properly.

117 Put the post in place. Use wood glue to bond the bottom of the post to the carving. After the glue dries, scrape off any excess with the hobby knife.

118 Three posts hold up the porch roof, but if you simply divide the distance between the posts by two, they won't be in perspective. Find the position for the center post by measuring along the fascia line in the drawing.

119 Carve the second post just as you did the first one. Since it is farther away from your eye, its dimensions are narrower than the first post.

120 Position the last porch post and add the dock posts. Place the dock posts under the porch using the same insertion methods described in Steps 114 through 117.

121 The sash bars are made from a two-ply composition using very thin pieces of mahogany veneer, which can be purchased at many home centers or from woodworking supply catalogs, glued together. When laminating the veneer, arrange each ply so that the grain is unidirectional. Apply an ample amount of yellow woodworking glue to one surface of each ply of veneer. Then place both of those surfaces together.

122 Clamp the veneers together between two pieces of wood to exert even pressure. Wax the clamping boards so that any glue squeeze-out won't cause the veneers to stick to the boards.

123 One piece of veneer is too thin and unstable, but two pieces laminated together, while strong and stable, are too thick. Use a belt sander to reduce the plys to the thickness of one piece of veneer.

TIP: When belt-sanding the veneer, use a block of scrap wood to apply even pressure across the section being sanded. Alternate between both sides with equal amounts of sanding time. The objective is to get two micro-thin layers of wood with a glue joint in the middle. Periodically hold the veneer up with a high intensity light behind it to see if the wood is being sanded evenly.

124 Use the miniature circular saw attached to a flexible shaft tool handpiece to cut the sanded veneer by rip-sawing along the length of the grain. Once again, use the drawing to measure how wide the pieces are cut.

125 Cut the veneer to length with the hobby knife. Put a drop of glue on each end and then press the veneer in place. There is no need to worry about the veneer shifting if the wood expands and contracts because the pieces of wood are so small.

126 Sash bars are placed in two sections. Use the hobby knife to put a drop of glue in place.

127 Push the left side of the sash bar into the glue with the point of the hobby knife.

TIP: Tweezers can be helpful in handling these small pieces of wood; however, even they can become cumbersome. A hobby knife with a sharp-pointed no. 11 blade can be used to lightly "stab" the piece of wood perpendicular to its grain to pick it up. Once the piece is in place with glue, twist the blade lightly and the piece of wood will release from the point.

128 Use a drawing to duplicate the correct proportions of the shutters. Note that the perspective from which you see the house means that shutters are not square or rectangular, but trapezoidal in shape.

129 The shutters are also cut from the laminated, sanded veneer. Bond each shutter in place using a small drop of glue in the middle of the component only. This allows both the top and the bottom of the shutter to "float."

130 After the glue dries, use the pencil grinder to cut a series of small V cuts. These cuts create the effect of louvers in the shutters.

131 Use sanded veneer for the bulrushes as well. Consecutive angled cuts form the top of one bulrush and the bottom of another. With this method, you can get several rushes out of one strip of veneer. Use the drawing to determine their sizes and make sure you put some taper into the bulrushes.

TIP: When making very small pieces, it is helpful to work on a white piece of shirt cardboard. Its contrasting surface makes them easier to see. The cardboard also provides for a good cutting surface.

132 Create a small angled tab ¹⁄₁₆ in. long on the bottom of the bulrush. The tab is used to glue the bulrush to the carving. To make the tab, push a bend in the veneer using the dull backside of the hobby blade. The shirt cardboard cushions the bending process and the veneer is less likely to break.

133 Put a small drop of glue on the surface of the scene using the drawing as a guide. A toothpick works well for this task. Place the tab of the bulrush into the glue. Then using the hobby knife with the tip of the blade broken off, press and hold it in place for a few moments. After a few minutes, the small drop of glue will be dry enough to hold it in place.

134 Add additional bulrushes until you are pleased with the results.

135 The final step is to use the conical aluminum oxide stone to remove the "step" from the bottoms of the bulrushes so the tabs blend into the carving. Make sure the glue is totally dry before doing this.

Finishing and Framing

136 The extra ½ in. of wood used for clamping is removed with a bandsaw. Use clear satin acrylic spray to evenly coat the carving front and back. Make sure to spray in all directions to cover the entire carving, especially where it has been backcut. Three thin coats are better than one heavy coat to make sure that the spray does not run.

137 After the coating to dry, it is ready for the final touch of framing. Note how the acrylic gives the water a reflective quality by creating glare from its luster.

138 A pleasing way to frame the relief carving is to use ¾-in. by 2-in. pieces of mahogany with mitered corners. The inside dimensions of the frame should be ⅛ in. larger than the carving. The extra wood allows the carving to expand and contract with seasonal humidity changes without the miter joints fracturing. An inner liner to the frame can consist of ¼-in. by 2¼-in. pieces of another wood such as cherry. The liner hides the gap caused by the carving being smaller than the frame. Do not glue pieces in place yet.

139 Remove the liner from the frame and trace each of the four sides of the carving to the corresponding part of the liner. Make sure you have both the liner and the carving flat against the workbench.

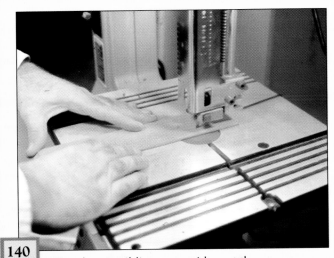

140 Using the pencil line as a guide, cut the excess wood from the bottom of the liner with the bandsaw.

141 Once the liner is cut, place the finished carving inside the frame for a trial fit.

142 After making sure that all four pieces fit together with the miters lining up, glue them in place. Spring clamps will hold them while the glue dries. It is a good idea to remove any excess glue while it is still wet. After the glue dries, give the entire frame a final sanding and apply three coats of the satin acrylic.

143 The carving is then inserted into the frame. It is held in place with two ¼-in. by 1⅛-in. pieces of a wood such as cherry screwed into the frame—not the carving.

144 The addition of a small picture lamp enhances the shadows and highlights.

Lighthouse Line Pattern

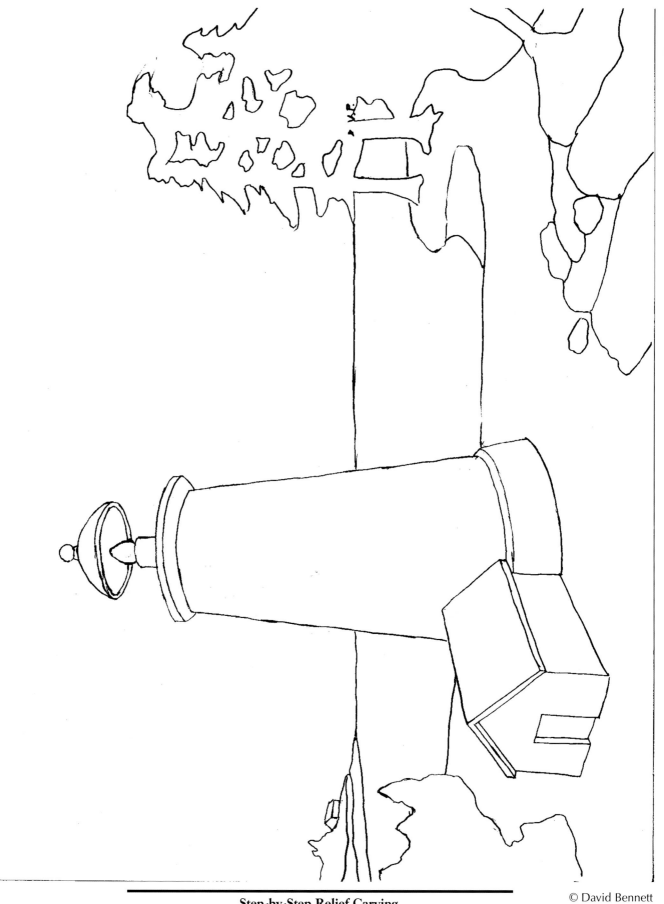

Lighthouse Illustration Pattern

A Helpful Reference

I often use as a reference with my students a book titled *Perspective*, by Vredeman de Vries (Dover Publications, Inc.), an architect-engraver who lived in Holland in the 16th century. His influence throughout Northern Europe was widespread. His many engravings opened up new avenues of architectural representation.

As the title suggests, this is a book devoted to perspective drawings. My students find it helpful to clearly seeing how a master used horizon lines and vanishing points in his drawings. While some of the illustrations are fairly complex, with multiple architectural elements, others are simpler in detail.

Included here are several of his drawings. While you may not wish to use any of his engravings as a relief carving subject, you will no doubt find them helpful in understanding how perspective changes as objects get farther away from sight, even in a two-dimensional drawing.

Perspective Translation — That is, the Most famous art of eyesight, which looks upon or through objects, on a painted wall, panel or canvas; in which are shown certain ancient as well as modern buildings, Temples or Shrines, Palaces, Private Apartments, Porticos, Streets, Promenades, Gardens, Marketplaces, Roads and other such constructions, resting on their fundamental lines, their basis being clearly explained with descriptions; an art of the greatest utility and necessity for all Painters, Engravers, Sculptors, Metalworkers, Architects, Designers, Masons, Cabinetmakers, Carpenters and all lovers of art who may wish to apply themselves to this art with greater pleasure and less pain.
By Jan Vredeman de Vries [the Frisian, or Frieslander].
Engraved and legally published by Henricus Hondius Leiden

Step-by-Step Relief Carving

Perspective Study 1

Two focal points determine the perspective on these three rectangles.

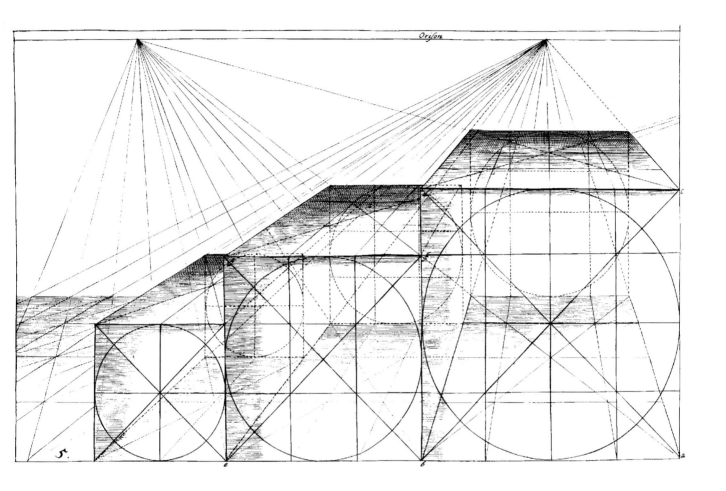

Perspective Study 2

Converging lines give the illusion of depth.

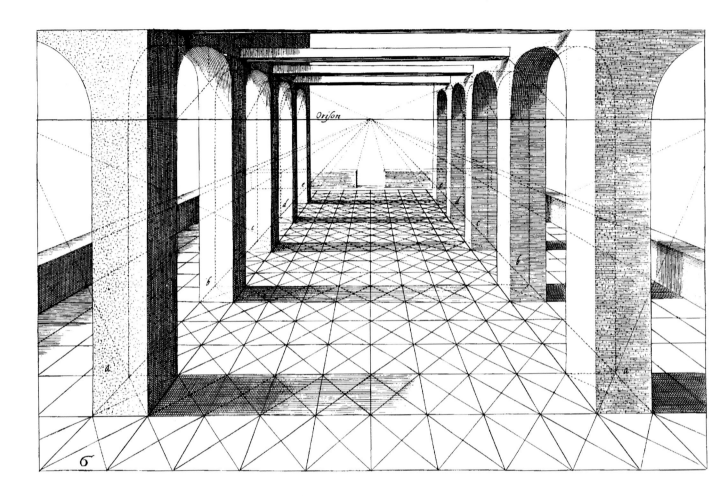

Perspective Study 3

All objects in an illustration need to be drawn with the same perspective.